THE LITTLE BOOK OF CALM

D6646118

PAUL WILSON

A PLUME BOOK

Plume
Published by the Penguin Group
Penguin Books USA Inc., 375 Hudson Street, New York, New York 10014, U.S.A.
Penguin Books Ltd, 27 Wrights Lane, London W8 5TZ, England
Penguin Books, Australia Ltd, Ringwood, Victoria, Australia
Penguin Books Canada Ltd, 10 Alcorn Avenue, Toronto, Ontario, Canada M4V 3B2
Penguin Books (N.Z.) Ltd 182–190 Wairau Road, Auckland 10, New Zealand

Penguin Books Ltd, Registered Offices: Harmondsworth, Middlesex, England

Published by Plume, an imprint of Dutton Signet, a division of Penguin Books USA Inc. First published in Australia by Penguin Books Australia Ltd.

First Plume Printing, January, 1997
10 9 8 7 6 5 4 3 2 1

Copyright © Paul Wilson, 1996
All rights reserved

REGISTERED TRADEMARK—MARCA REGISTRADA

LIBRARY OF CONGRESS CATALOGING-IN-PUBLICATION DATA:

Printed in the United States of America

Without limiting the rights under copyright reserved above, no part of this publication may be reproduced, stored in or introduced into a retrieval system, or transmitted, in any form or by any means (electronic, mechanical, photocopying, recording or otherwise), without the prior written permission of both the copyright owner and the above publisher of this book.

BOOKS ARE AVAILABLE AT QUANTITY DISCOUNTS WHEN USED TO PROMOTE PRODUCTS OR SERVICES. FOR INFORMATION PLEASE WRITE TO PREMIUM MARKETING DIVISION, PENGUIN BOOKS USA INC., 375 HUDSON STREET, NEW YORK, NEW YORK 10014.

I've written this little book to be an on-hand comfort to you. Carry it with you to steal moments of peace and tranquillity. At any time, in any place.

Follow its recommendations and you will remain calm. Even in the most difficult moments.

And, most useful of all, when you feel troubled simply let this book fall open – let your intuition guide you – and you will see the most effective way for you to find calm at that particular moment.

Trust your intuition and you will become calm.

Carry a Piece of the Quiet

Concentrate on silence.
When it comes, dwell on what
it sounds like.

Then strive to carry
that quiet with you
wherever you go.

WASTE SOME TIME

Hard-working people never waste time on frivolous, fun-filled activities. Yet, for hard-working people, *any* time spent this way is far from wasted.

SELECT YOUR COMPANY WELL

As harsh as it may sound, mixing with highly stressed people will make you feel stressed.

On the other hand, mixing with calm people – even for the briefest period – will leave you feeling calm.

Be captivated by your breath

When you dwell on the sound of your breathing, when you can really hear it coming and going, peace will not be far behind.

Pause between changes

There's always a temptation to lump all your life changes into one big masochistic event.

Do your stress levels a favour and take on changes one at a time.

INVEST IN A FRUIT BOWL

The more beautiful your fruit bowl, the better stocked it is, the less likely you are to turn to stress-enhancing snack foods.

Eat more fruit, and you'll feel more relaxed – it's as sweet as that.

Disregard small issues

The most important skill in staying calm is not to lose sleep over small issues. The second most important skill is to be able to view *all* issues as small issues.

START TEN MINUTES EARLY

Start every journey ten minutes early. Not only will you avoid the stress of haste, but if all goes well you'll have ten minutes to relax before your next engagement.

Worry when the time comes

Most worries are future-based. They revolve around things that, in most cases, will *never* happen.

Concentrate on the present and the future will take care of itself.

Sip a Peppermint

If you substitute a herbal tea such as peppermint for more stimulating drinks such as coffee and tea, your ability to be calm will be enhanced many times.

ADMIT YOU FEEL CALM

If you want to trick your subconscious into helping you feel calm, simply repeat: 'Every moment I feel calmer and calmer.'

Wear sensible shoes

Any reflexologist will tell you that true relaxation begins at the feet. It seems obvious, but wearing comfortable shoes is nearly as relaxing as wearing no shoes at all.

SEEK THE BEST IN EVERYTHING

Make a practice of looking for the best in people and situations. You'll find that simple approach induces optimism and positivity – both of which lead to calm.

BRUSH OR BE BRUSHED

Take the time to brush someone's hair. Better still, brush your own – or have someone else do it. Slowly, methodically, extensively. (It massages several calming acupressure points,
and the repetition works wonders.)

PRETEND YOU'RE HUMAN

Leave it to others to be perfect, to be wonderful. Be content with what you are – you'll be much more relaxed as a result.

Start Christmas now

It probably took a lot of trial and error over the centuries, but Christmas carols and lullabies have a unique ability to soothe.

Use them (silently) all year round.

SINGLE OUT SIMPLE PLEASURES

Approach something with your full attention and an open mind, and you'll find pleasure and complexity in it. A bunch of grapes. Or a glass of water. Or a field of grass. Or a sky of clouds.

All of such things can lead to calm.

JETTISON THE PAST

There is seldom any rational reason for having regrets about past deeds or events. Because the past does not exist in any way other than in your memory.

When you recognise this lack of reality, you can be calm.

Take junior lessons

Take a lesson in calmness from children: watch how they live every moment for the pleasure of the moment.

Pretend, and you could be like that, too.

THINK CALM

Have calm thoughts.
Picture calm scenes.
Recall calm sounds.

And guess what you'll be feeling ...

Steal thirty seconds

When you're tense, go somewhere quiet – even the bathroom will do at a pinch – and take thirty seconds to gather your thoughts, and work out how you're going to become calm.

They could be the most useful thirty seconds in your day.

CLEAR OUT THE CLUTTER

Physical disarray adds
to the tension of life.
Clearing out the clutter
is an orderly way to calm.

Stimulate with intent

Recognise that there is a time for stimulation and a time for calm. This means never trying to fool yourself that a stimulant can help you to relax.

Spray orange blossom

Add three drops of orange blossom oil (neroli) to a cup of mineral water, and spray it from an atomiser when you need to feel relaxed.

Ignore small print

Small print is custom-designed to induce frustration. If you want to stay calm, have someone else read (and explain) the small type for you.

Pat something

Share your life with a pet – being generous with your affection to it – and you'll have an appreciative assistant in your efforts to become calm.

Forgive on the spot

To bear ill-feelings towards someone else is more damaging to the bearer than the recipient.

For your own sake, forgive quickly and freely.

BARRICADE THE DOOR

There comes a time when you need to shut yourself off from interruption, to concentrate on your own needs and responsibilities.

Do it for at least one hour a day.

LEVITATE

Stand straighter and taller than you believe feels natural, with an *imaginary* thread attached to the top of your skull lifting you a few millimetres above the ground.

The higher above the ground you feel, the closer you will be to feeling calm.

TOUCH OR BE TOUCHED

The human touch is one of the surest ways of unburdening stresses. Just as the embrace of a parent soothes the upset child, just as a kiss or handshake takes the sting out of an argument, the simplest touch sometimes works miracles.

Paint the town green

Plants pour oxygen into the environment while soaking up carbon dioxide and pollutants. Keep plants where you work, sleep and live, and you'll enjoy more oxygen.

The more oxygen you can get, the calmer you will become.

Look for the pleasure in calm

Unlike muscle building, techniques for creating calm work better when there is no pain, no effort.

In fact, being calm is in itself one of life's great pleasures.

Unwind with an Aphrodisiac

Ginseng, which has been coveted for its aphrodisiac properties for centuries, also has a reputation for being able to relax the nervous system if taken regularly.

Lower the Crossbar

One of the greatest strains in life is constantly having to live up to the standards we set for ourselves.

Do yourself a favour and – from time to time – relax those standards a little.

Learn two Tai Chi exercises

It is almost impossible to feel tense when you're concentrating on a Tai Chi routine.

Learn the basic Tai Chi exercises and you have a secret to becoming calm.

Listen for the Quiet

Quiet is the essence of calm. You cannot *force* quiet, you can only accept it when it comes. But if you listen for it, really listen, you will find it in the most unexpected places.

All it takes is a little concentration.

Rest your fingers

Gently rest the thumb and fingertips of one hand against the corresponding thumb and fingertips of the other. Just the lightest touch. Breathe slowly for sixty seconds and allow the calm to overtake you.

Wear white

The clothes you wear have a distinct influence on the way you feel. Loose garments, natural fabrics and light colours all lead to calm.

This is why yogis wear white.

Sell your wristwatch

Have you ever noticed how relaxed you feel the moment you remove your watch? Remove yours from time to time, and remove yourself from time pressures.

Be negative about ions

Negative ions are remarkable things. They freshen the air, assist your breathing, enhance your mood and induce feelings of calm and energy.

All it takes is a low-cost negative ion generator (ioniser). Or an electrical storm.

Rub on a Rose

Massage is one of the most pleasurable ways to be soothed into a state of relaxation. By adding a little rose oil to your massage oil you can make the experience doubly effective.

Make for the Straight Back

Oddly enough, the chairs that help you relax most may not be the lazy, over-stuffed variety that immediately springs to mind. A chair that supports your back, and helps you to sit erect, is probably your best choice.

Declare today a holiday

Imagine every day is a holiday. Do one little thing that stimulates this holiday mood each day, then watch your worries fade away.

Play a calm role

Pretend you are calm: adopt the characteristics of a calm person, pretend that others see you as a calm person, and in no time you'll be a calm person.

Run for your life

Running is one of life's antidotes to stress. It's simple, requires no special training and it begins to take effect within the first 200 metres.

Reflect on beauty

Do this, not for the stimulation, but for the elevation. Because you'll find calm where you find beauty – regardless of whether it is natural or man-made.

Sleep like a baby

Anything that interferes with your sleep – coffee, cola, alcohol – interferes with your ability to become calm.

Do whatever is necessary to get as much sleep as you feel you need.

Stride for Sheer Delight

While some forms of exercise may seem torturous, walking is easy and pleasurable. Walk every day – not because you have to, but because if you combine it with the right attitude, it can be the most relaxing way to get from A to B.

Snatch a couple of minutes

If you feel you need it, take brief cat naps throughout the day. You'll be surprised at how much peace can come from a couple of minutes – even while sitting at your typewritezzzzzzzz

zzzzzzzzzzzzzzzzzzzzzzzzzzzz

zzzzzzzzzzzzzz

zzzzzzz

START IN THE RAW

Start every meal with something raw – fruit or vegetables. Not only do these 'alkaline foods' enhance feeling of calm, they add harmony to a meal.

Pamper your feet

Soak your feet, then massage them with moisturiser or a relaxing combination of essential oils.

You'll be blissfully relaxed in no time.

Take the back seat

However much you think you might enjoy driving, it is a stressful business. Take the back seat (with a driver you trust), and spend the journey sharing your calm.

Control only what you can control

Be rigorous in differentiating between what is achievable and what is a waste of time. Then devote your energies only to those tasks you can achieve (pass on the others to someone else).

SIMPLIFY

The fewer things you must do in life, the fewer things you own, manage or are responsible for, the fewer are the stresses that accompany them.

Resort to politeness

Practise politeness, not for the benefit of others, but for the ennoblement of yourself. It doesn't matter if the receivers reciprocate (which they usually will) or not – you will feel better for your niceness.

RECOGNISE THE DIFFERENCE BETWEEN HAVING AND LIVING

THINK WARM

A cold body is seldom calm. Rubbing the hands together, furiously, helps you to feel warm.

Feeling calm follows feeling warm.

Develop a Taste for Fish

Why are fish so relaxing to watch? Because they move slowly and, perhaps more importantly, because they breathe slowly.

Merely watching them is like gazing on a seascape.

Picture yourself

Picture yourself on an idyllic South Pacific island. See yourself on the sun-bleached sands. Note what you're wearing, the relaxed way you're standing, the way the breeze blows your hair, the calm, semi-smile on your face.

Now imagine what it *feels* like to be there.

Take a long cut

There's nothing like a change to break the stress patterns that build throughout the day. Every now and then make a point of doing something you wouldn't normally do – like taking a different route home from work.

Use the time to appreciate the change.

Plan your worries

Put aside a certain amount of time each day – at the same time each day – which you devote to sorting through your worries.

When the time is up, stop worrying.

Massage your temples

Some of the most powerful calming acupressure points can be found at the temples. Apply a light pressure as you breathe out, ease the pressure as you breathe in.

Be positive about being positive

Work on having positive thoughts, pay particular attention to speaking positive words, then let the resultant positive feelings take care of everything else.

TURTLE

The pace you move has a direct relationship with the way you feel. Slow down your movements, consciously relax your gestures and expressions, and before you know it you'll be relaxed.

DISCOVER

It's hard to feel tense when you're learning something you want to know.

And you can learn from the most unlikely places.

Finger the Beads

Use up the nervous energy that concentrates in the fingers and hands by fingering worry beads.

MAKE LOVE

The relaxation that follows love-making works on many different levels.

Ignore the phone once

You only have to leave a phone ringing once or twice in your life to appreciate that important calls always ring back.

One less pressure in your life.

Go limp

Really tense one set of muscles – such as the arms or legs – then quickly let them go limp. The contrast between 'tense' and 'relaxed' should indicate what 'relaxed' really feels like.

Dwell on that feeling.

FIND WONDER IN ALL YOU DO

There is little doubt that those who get the most from life are those who look for the wonder in even the smallest things they do. Cultivate this skill and you'll find peace and satisfaction as well.

Recognise addiction

Satisfying cravings of any kind (nicotine, chocolate, caffeine, alcohol) is no way to help yourself feel calm. Recognise addictions for what they are, and find an alternative.

Then you can be calm.

Sip Warm Water

A glass of chilled water will calm you more than most other liquids.

A cup of *warm* water will calm you even more.

Take a Long Distance View

Your eyes are at their most relaxed when they focus on distant scenes – especially natural ones.

And when your eyes are relaxed, your body starts to relax.

Face a Wet Towel

As any beauty therapist or barber will tell you, nothing soaks away facial stress and tension quite so efficiently as a damp, hot towel.

Go on, smile

A smile relaxes all the major facial muscles. It also sets off an emotional chain reaction that invariably helps you feel good.

Accept only one deadline

Deadlines are at the root of so many stress problems. Take on only one deadline at a time, and you will become master of your own time.

Float

Float in a swimming pool, a float tank, or even a bathtub, and weightlessly feel your tensions dissolve.

MAKE MAGNANIMITY A HABIT

Indulge yourself by being generous – help someone out, perform an act of kindness, offer a compliment.

The person who will feel most uplifted by you having done so is ... you.

Go from A to B

While vitamin A foods enhance your ability to feel calm, it is the vitamin B foods that are known to have the most dynamic effect. Include beans, lentils, peas, nuts, seeds, wheatgerm, wholegrains, dairy foods in your diet.

Know when to withdraw

There comes a time in every struggle when determination serves no purpose and becomes an end unto itself.

Knowing when to move on to the next issue is a skill possessed by many calm people.

Reaffirm your friendships

If you tend to get overly serious about your work or your responsibilities, remind yourself that the most common deathbed regrets relate to neglected relationships, not unfinished business.

Turn off the lights

When all else fails in a stressful day, go somewhere quiet and dark, and listen to your breathing as you ease into a state of relaxation.

Dictate the Pace

Just as a group attitude or mood can influence the individual, a determined individual can influence the group. By moving slowly, speaking calmly, you can spread a feeling of calm within a group.

Practise saying no

There is only so much you can achieve before affecting your efficiency and state of mind.

Only take on what you can do – then politely, but firmly, turn down all other requests.

WRITE DOWN YOUR WORRY

It's marvellous how quickly many worries dissolve when you write them down on a piece of paper – then review the likelihood of them eventuating.

Nine times out of ten that likelihood will be remote.

Put your feet up

There's more to the simple act of putting your feet up than improved circulation.

It quickly leads to feelings of relaxation.

Stockpile Beautiful Moments

Write them down, keep a photo, keep a record in your computer. Then recall these moments often, reflecting on them, taking pleasure in them, integrating them into your day-to-day routine and outlook.

Grow your own

Gardeners are among the most calm and relaxed people (while they're gardening) you'll find.

Set your own agenda

If you set your own agenda, and don't allow others to dictate your pace too much, you will have much more time to become calm.

Caress the back of your hand

In Zone Therapy, the backs of the hands are the way to tap into calm. The lightest possible upwards stroke with the fingertips helps to induce a relaxed state.

PRUNE PRESSURE PHRASES

Pressure phrases like 'I have to', 'I must', 'I should', 'I don't have the time', exacerbate feelings of stress. Listen for such words in your thoughts and speech, then replace them with more relaxed phrases – 'I may', 'I choose to', 'I will make the time'.

Have little successes

There's nothing like a degree of success to help you become relaxed. Even if it's only with the most trivial activities, make room for yourself to succeed from time to time.

WATCH OUT FOR TENSE PEOPLE

Learn to recognise signs of tension and anxiety in others. In this way you can be aware of your own physiology, and can work towards becoming calm.

Appreciate the routine

Any task you can do on remote control has potential as a way of helping you to feel good. Treat it as a meditation, concentrating wholly on the moment, and you will be fulfilled.

Breathe less

A deeply relaxed person breathes only 5–8 times a minute. By slowing your breathing down to that rate, you will quickly relax.

ADD A DAB OF LAVENDER

A dab of lavender not only eases aches and pains, but works wonders in helping you to relax.

Rediscover Milk

Mother was right! Milk helps you to relax and become calm. (It is rich in calcium, a muscle relaxant, as well as an amino acid called tryptophan, a powerful natural sedative.)

Pretend You Believe

Regardless of what you know, by pretending to be absolutely calm and relaxed, you will fool your subconscious into believing you are calm and relaxed.

Wear Donald Duck underpants

Choose a few childlike accoutrements to remind you of the irreverent, uninhibited, joyous side of life.

Make your work important

The difference between abject drudgery and noble, uplifting work is often no more than perspective.

Treat your work as important, and the satisfaction that flows will work towards helping you unwind.

Bicker on schedule

While it's impossible to avoid all conflict and arguments, it *is* possible not to feel too bad when they happen. Simply postpone the argument.

Agree to discuss the issues in detail, at some later date ... and be surprised at how peacefully that can happen.

SHAMPOO SANS SHAMPOO

You access the calming acupressure points at the top of the head in the most pleasurable way through scalp massage – the actions of a shampoo, but without the shampoo.

Gaze on something blue

Or pink. Sometimes green.
Each of these colours – one warm, two cool – has the magical ability to instil calm in a troubled mind.

Rest in a Tub

A leisurely, warm bath soothes like no other method. Lower the lights, add a few drops of your favourite oil, and you'll be transported.

Love the moment

When you concentrate your attention on absorbing every detail of every moment – savouring every taste, hearing every sound, noting every colour – you will be calm before you know it.

Train a calm place

If you practise being calm in a certain place – say, a favourite chair or park bench – soon your subconscious will associate feelings of calm with that particular place.

Then simply go there to become calm.

Know when to stop

For most activities in life, there are no prizes for perseverance. When you know your stress levels are rising, stop what you're doing – either take a break or do something else.

SPREAD BEAUTY

Wherever you go in life, whatever you do, make a conscious effort to add a little beauty, or to contribute to the beauty that's already there.

Offer a compliment

You'll find the good feelings that flow from it will be as much yours as the recipient's.

TAKE ALL THE TIME IN THE WORLD

Contrary to what you may tell yourself, you have all the time in the world to do whatever you choose.

What cannot be fitted into your day, cannot be done – forget about it.

DELEGATE RUTHLESSLY

The more you delegate, the more comfortable and capable you become with the practice.

Then, the more you delegate, the less pressure you have to live with.

THANK YOUR GOOD HUMOUR

Get on speaking terms with your humour. Play games with it. Access it more than you think is a good thing ... and it will help you to become calm.

Massage your eyebrows

You do this intuitively when under pressure – now you can do it consciously. Work the relaxing acupressure points around the forehead by massaging your eyebrows in an outwards direction.

Learn to Love Change

If you appreciate that as much good comes from change as bad, you will avoid the concerns that many people seem to have about it.

Relax and be open to change when it visits.

Sleep on a patchouli pillow

Add three drops of patchouli or chamomile oils to your pillow every few nights for a blissfully calm sleep.

Shed a few tears

There is something both emotionally and physically soothing about crying.

VISUALISE A SUNSET

Even though sunsets may sometimes be sad, they are always peaceful.

And pink ones are even more peaceful.

Break the Pattern

When you find yourself under pressure, do something different. Stand where you wouldn't normally stand, sit where you wouldn't normally sit, think the way you wouldn't normally think.

SAY YOUR PRAYERS

If you have spiritual or religious beliefs, you probably have access to one of the world's most time-honoured methods of achieving tranquillity: prayer.

PRETEND IT'S SATURDAY

SWITCH OFF OR SWITCH ON

Electric lights, television, computers, fluorescent lights ... all add to feelings of tension.

Ironically, you can compensate for them with another electronic implement – an ioniser.

Be up for the sunrise

It is no coincidence that serious meditators, yogis, ascetics, martial artists, and many religious orders treat the moments before sunrise as the most precious of the day.

TAKE TO THE WAVES

Sea air, salt water and the sound of waves – all contribute to a growing sense of calm.

Get it off your chest

Articulating your problems often takes you half the way to solving them. Share your feelings and problems with someone else and you will feel more peaceful.

Make friends with a masseur

Or a beauty therapist.

Be conscious of choices

Whether you recognise them or not, you usually have choices. The art is to recognise them.

Because when you can see your choices, you will feel free.

THINK BEFORE YOU BUY

To avoid the stresses of debt, think about what you can afford to spend, long before you think about what you'd like to buy.

Sweat

Physical exertion counters the negative effects of stress and helps you to feel good about yourself.

Exercise until there is a light film of sweat on your brow, then continue for twenty more minutes.

Hold the words back

When you're under pressure, words come quickly and the rhythm of your speech speeds up. By reversing these patterns – slowing your words, articulating your thoughts more carefully, slowing your breathing – you can beguile your subconscious into believing you are relaxed.

Calm down your diet

If you want to feel calm, eat more raw fruit and vegetables, yoghurt, milk, eggs, wholegrains, beans, pulses, nuts and seeds.

Watch your head

Most stress and anxiety is the result of what happens inside your head, rather than what happens to your body.

Take comfort in the fact that most things which take place in your thoughts *never* eventuate.

Leave town

It is more relaxing to walk down a country road than a suburban street. It is more comforting to gaze on rolling hills than on rolling stock.

It is more relaxing to sail in the wide open sea than it is on a busy harbour.

Smell the Blooms

Certain scents stimulate the production of the relaxing chemical, serotonin, in the brain.

Among the more effective of these scents are lavender and chamomile.

Appreciate life in 3/4 time

Not only is the waltz one of the most lighthearted and joyous of musical forms, it can also be the most soothing.

Think 3/4 time as you walk, and feel the joy in your step.

Sit in a church

Regardless of what you believe in, churches and temples are extraordinary places of peace.

Take a pew and absorb the atmosphere of absolute peace and calm that permeates them.

Press on the roof

Tense people have tense jaw muscles. To relieve this tension, simply press on the roof of the mouth, behind the front teeth, with your tongue.

Turn into a windmill

Imagine a windmill turning. Copy those actions with your arms, transcribing a great slow-motion arc – and you will wave yourself calm.

Frown Darkly

Tighten your forehead and eyebrows into a tight, ugly frown. Then raise your eyebrows and feel the tension lift.

Remember the feeling of relaxation that follows.

Dance till you drop

One of the most pleasurable exercises around, uninhibited dancing distracts even the most committed worrier.

Cover your face

Place the palm of a hand on each side of your face – from your lips to your eyes, allowing room for your nose – and apply a light pressure until you feel relaxed.

SHELVE YOUR WORRIES

Decide on a way of storing your worries each evening before you go to bed. Whisper them into an envelope or write them in a diary, then store and forget them.

Chances are they'll be greatly reduced, if not solved, by morning.

Eat 80:20

The ideal calm diet maintains a ratio of alkalines (wholegrains, cereals, vegetables, etc.) to acids (coffee, meat, sugar, processed foods, preservatives, etc.) of about 80:20.

Bach to the Rescue

The most well-known Bach treatment, Rescue Remedy, produces a calming effect in trying situations as diverse as major traumas through to little anxieties.

Anything for a Laugh

Remain on the lookout for things that make you laugh – and, if you see nothing worth laughing at, *pretend* you see it.

Then laugh.

Write it down

Write down your concerns and be surprised at how quickly they dissolve when you read them on paper.

Make an appointment

Make an appointment with yourself to deal with worries at a specific time in the future.

The more seriously you treat that appointment, the more efficiently you'll deal with the problem.

EMPLOY YOUR SUBCONSCIOUS

Your subconscious specialises in finding solutions to your most personal problems.

Place your faith in it, and give your conscious mind a rest.

MEDITATE

Concentrate on a movement, a sound, an image, a thought – without strain and without concern if your attention wanders.

Before you know it, you will be meditating.

Avoid cogs twice a day

Twice a day, spend a few minutes not being a cog in the machine – take a walk around the block, have a nap under the desk, deliver the mail to the post office, abandon your routine – it will add variety and vitality to your day.

GIVE YOURSELF PERMISSION

Find a quiet place, regularly, and say out loud: 'For five minutes in every hour, I give myself permission to relax and to be calm.'

Keep repeating it to yourself.

Only worry about big things

If you can overlook the small issues of life, and concentrate on the important ones, you will be much closer to calm.

Alight one stop early

If you consciously set out to break your own routines, you can also break your worry habits. Take a different road home, get off the bus a stop early, talk to a stranger, and absorb the differences.

CHANGE

There are only two ways to handle tense situations: you can change them, or you can change the way you look at them.

There is enlightenment to be had in changing the way you look at things.

Use a soft voice

Have you ever noticed a calm person with a loud voice?

Be nice

As unfashionable as the sentiment may seem, nice people find fewer impediments to becoming calm.

About the Author

Paul Wilson thrives in several high-stress worlds: chairman of an advertising agency, strategic consultant to some of Australia's major corporations, director of a hospital, and father to a teenager and two young children. Instead of focusing on stress he has become an authority on calm, and is the author of two bestselling books, *Instant Calm* and *The Calm Technique*.

E-mail him on: paulwil@calmcentre.com.au